# QUESTIONS
### FOR
# DEEP
# THINKERS

# QUESTIONS

## *FOR*

# DEEP THINKERS

## 200+ OF THE MOST CHALLENGING QUESTIONS YOU (PROBABLY) NEVER THOUGHT TO ASK

HENRY KRAEMER AND BRANDON MARCUS

Adams Media
An Imprint of Simon & Schuster, Inc.
57 Littlefield Street
Avon, Massachusetts 02322

First Adams Media trade paperback edition MARCH 2018

ADAMS MEDIA and colophon are trademarks of Simon and Schuster.

For information about special discounts for bulk purchases, please contact Simon & Schuster Special Sales at 1-866-506-1949 or business@simonandschuster.com.

The Simon & Schuster Speakers Bureau can bring authors to your live event. For more information or to book an event contact the Simon & Schuster Speakers Bureau at 1-866-248-3049 or visit our website at www.simonspeakers.com.

Manufactured in the United States of America

10 9 8 7 6 5 4 3 2 1

Library of Congress Cataloging-in-Publication Data has been applied for.

ISBN 978-1-5072-0712-3
ISBN 978-1-5072-0713-0 (ebook)

# DEDICATION

To our partners, parents, and pals for putting up with questions like these for many years before we had a good excuse.

# CONTENTS

# INTRODUCTION

"Would you rather have pirates or Vikings house-sit for you?"

"If a werewolf landed on the moon, would it touch down as a person or a wolf?"

"Is it better for your home to be haunted by a stranger or a family member?"

If these questions send your thoughts racing and shift your hand into chin-stroking position, welcome to your new favorite book. *Questions for Deep Thinkers* is your shortcut to genius. Here you will find more than two hundred questions—with topics ranging from philosophy and literature to the social sciences and the arts—all guaranteed to transform your dinner table or dorm room into a hip debate society. After all, where else are you going to find a reason to ponder which dinosaur is least likely to kill you; what would have happened if Romeo and Juliet met online; or whether Picasso would have enjoyed Mr. Potato Head? And if you're not sure how to even begin answering these questions, don't worry! We don't expect you to have all the answers, so each chapter begins with a sample debate to chart the way.

As the renowned deep thinker Socrates said, "The unexamined life is not worth living." (Indeed, one could imagine him writing this type of book were it not for his unfortunate hemlock-drinking habit.) So read on, open your mind, and get ready to examine life's greatest mysteries—or, you know, just have a fun night answering some genius-level questions with your friends.

# PHILOSOPHY FOR DEEP THINKERS

True deep thinkers are hot for philosophy. Philosophers ask big questions. They ponder humanity. They wear togas. (We can offer you the first two, and you can take care of the third with a bedsheet and a few safety pins.) By the end of this chapter you'll have explored enduring mysteries. Are vampires annoyed by mosquitoes? Do ghosts surf the web? How ripped would you get enduring eternal labor in Hell? Philosopher René Descartes once said, "I think, therefore I am." So read on and be somebody!

# Can ghosts choose who they haunt?

**POINT:** It is well established that ghosts are bound to a single set location for the course of their unfinished astral business. They're called "haunted houses," not "haunted Christines." Maybe in the fifties that meant a ghoul could haunt one family for decades or even a whole life. But in this economy? Ghosts are lucky if they can even get to know your name, sleeping schedule, and top three fears before you get evicted and they're on to a new hauntee. There's no stability for today's ghosts. Tragic, really.

**COUNTERPOINT:** You make it sound like being a ghost is akin to working the night shift at a hospital: just take whatever job comes up first. You're telling me that Ebenezer Scrooge just happened to encounter three ghosts who were perfectly suited for him? Heck no! Ghosts decide who to haunt, where to haunt, and what type of chain will make the best rattle. They look at all the possible hauntees and say, "Hey, I bet I can convince that guy to change his ways with some holiday-inspired life lessons!"

If a werewolf landed on the moon, would it touch down as a person or a wolf?

If a Sasquatch and a yeti met
in the wild, would they be able
to communicate?

# Do ghosts use the Internet?

# What do vampires think of mosquitoes?

Would Jesus prefer to celebrate Christmas or Easter?

It's the first dance at your wedding: would you rather have your former middle school self pick the song or possess your body and dance for you?

# Is dog Heaven the same as human Heaven?

Is it better to starve to death or be eaten alive by your favorite animal?

If you are sent to Hell to do eternal labor, does your body become muscular but rangy like a jacked old man's or does it grow stronger and stronger but always look slightly less fit?

Which is better: to know
that you will eventually drown
in a pool of your own sweat,
but never know when, or sweat
so much that your clothes
drip during every important
event of your life?

Did Noah want to eat any of the animals on the ark?

**Would you choose to become a world-famous rock star, along with all the glories that entails, if you could never hear music again?**

Is it better to be told the meaning of life as a baby or as an elderly person at death's door?

If human beings laid eggs, would people eat as many chicken eggs as they do today?

# Is a loincloth underwear?

# Could you shave a Sasquatch and pass it off as a professional athlete?

Would you rather have your worst grade school haircut forever or have the most embarrassing thing you ever wrote be read on national TV next to a picture of your face?

Who would be the best *Saturday Night Live* host: Jesus, Muhammad, or Buddha?

**Would you rather be the first person on earth or the last?**

Is it better to live to be two hundred years old and never know what day you'll die
or live to be one hundred years old and know the exact day you'll die?

**Is it better for your home to be haunted by a stranger or a family member?**

# Can vampires breathe in space?

# Would you let the Devil throw your bachelor party?

# Would you trade a life of celibacy for a lifelong orgasm?

# How old do you look in Heaven?

Is it better to be reincarnated as a gnat that lives for one day or as a tortoise that can live to be one hundred years old?

Would you rather give a presentation on the first day of sex ed and have to say everything you know going into it or on the last day and have to say everything you've learned?

# Would you invite Jesus to your Christmas party or Hanukkah party?

# Do cats and dogs share a Heaven?

Marry, coitus, kill: yourself at twenty-five, at fifty-five, at seventy-five?

# If angels are real, is it more likely that their wings are made of feathers or skin?

Which would be a better portal to another dimension: your front door every seventh time you use it or every restaurant bathroom in your town?

Given the choice of being reincarnated as a dog tomorrow or a human being at a random point in history, which would you choose?

Would you rather have your former middle school self choose what you wear every day or decide the theme music that follows you everywhere you go?

What's worse: an ice-cold shower every day or only one hot shower each month?

How much would you need to get paid to allow your dreams to be turned into a TV show?

They say that if you don't learn from history then you're doomed to repeat it. Well, we don't want to repeat anything. We are moving forward, and you're coming along with us whether you like it or not. So get your brain ready to investigate which invention makes people most miserable and decide which disgusting part of George Washington's body you would rather have. After all, history isn't just something you learn about in books. If you use your wits and imagination, you can relive history and maybe even change the future! (And if you get any good ideas from this chapter, you're legally obligated to share the profits with us.)

**What would make better reality TV: the Salem witch trials or the court of Henry VIII?**

**POINT:** As someone who has watched far too much reality TV, it's so painfully obvious that the Salem witch trials are far more suitable for the trashy genre that created *Survivor*, *Jersey Shore*, and *The Bachelor*. The trials featured all the hallmarks of good reality TV: accusations, betrayals, alliances, and death-defying (or not) aquatic challenges. The Salem witch trials were the first "court cases" that captured America's yearning for intrigue, and they would fit perfectly in our current TV landscape. If it aired today, I guarantee the ratings would be hot—on fire, even.

**COUNTERPOINT:** There are two things people love: dating shows and high stakes. With the court of Henry VIII, you get both in spades! This show has it all: a (much) larger than life groom-to-be who can eat a whole boar, drink a barrel of wine, and pick a fight with the pope—all before dinner; a line of eager women in flowing gowns, each competing for the chance to become queen of an entire country for the rest of her life (however long that may be); and a beautiful castle with high ceilings, gorgeous views, and a world-class ax collection. It's *The Bachelor* meets *Survivor*! People will lose their heads for this show.

**When humans milked another animal for the first time, did they squeeze it or suckle it?**

# Who would you prefer to be snowed in with: Charles Manson or Al Capone?

Which great invention has caused the most unhappiness: fire, the wheel, or the Internet?

**Marry, coitus, kill: Mary, Queen of Scots; Napoleon; Fidel Castro?**

# Would cavemen be proud of us for camping or think we're insane?

Who would be a more successful gunslinger in the American Wild West: Genghis Khan or Joan of Arc?

Would you rather have George Washington's teeth or his personal hygiene habits?

# Which president of the United States would win *The Bachelorette*?

Who would you rather see a muscular version of: Gandhi or Winston Churchill?

**Would medieval knights have been more intimidating riding motorcycles or elephants?**

**Which store would be kicked out of the mall first: an Orange Julius managed by Julius Caesar or an Old Navy managed by Christopher Columbus?**

Would you rather have pirates or Vikings house-sit for you?

Is it more likely that the United States faked the moon landing or covered up alien contact at Area 51?

# Which queen would you rather spend an afternoon with: Elizabeth I or Beyoncé?

Would you rather be a soldier during the American Civil War or a townsperson during the Black Death?

**Which would the world miss more if it had never been invented: diapers or paper?**

Who would find modern America most confusing: Americans from the 1920s, the 1940s, or the 1960s?

**Who would you rather add to your friend group: Nelson Mandela, Cleopatra, or Stephen Hawking?**

Would you rather go to a medieval doctor who specializes in bloodletting and leeches or a modern dentist who doesn't use anesthesia?

Who is more likely to be remembered in one hundred years: Lady Gaga, LeBron James, or Bill Gates?

**Would you rather have the power to relive and change any ten days over the course of your life or live ten days as a different person of your choice each day?**

Would you rather be a funeral director in ancient Egypt, medieval England, or revolutionary France?

If you could stop one assassination, whose would you choose: Archduke Franz Ferdinand's (whose murder started World War I) or Abraham Lincoln's (whose murder robbed America of four years of its greatest president and untold opportunities to repair the damage of slavery)?

Which would you rather get advice on from Sigmund Freud: Mother's Day gifts or first-date etiquette?

# CHAPTER 3
## LITERATURE FOR DEEP THINKERS

Books are all about questions. They force us to question our knowledge, our morals, and even the world around us. Nothing stimulates the mind more than a book. And as the years go on questions about literature pile up inside us. We can't keep them inside anymore, so we're spilling them all throughout this chapter. Is it better to be a Hogwarts student or an X-Man? What oddity of our modern world would be the best subject matter for a Shakespeare play? If these questions arouse your curiosity, then we have good news and bad news: this chapter is perfect for you and you're a lot like us, and nobody wants that.

After Humpty Dumpty has a great fall, the king sends all his horses and all his men to put Humpty back together again. Why would anybody send horses to put something back together?

**POINT:** The simplest answer here is that in the world of Humpty Dumpty, horses have hands. When you start with that assumption, using horses makes a ton of sense. It is unlikely that these horses would have had only one set of hands and then a set of hooves. It would only stand to reason that they had four hands, providing a significant advantage for reassembling a giant man-egg—the horse could hold Humpty together with his front hands and apply glue with his back hands. The real question is: why did the king's men even need to be involved?

**COUNTERPOINT:** First of all, you need to be sensitive when talking about horses and glue. Secondly, you need to approach this question from a more political angle. The king in Humpty Dumpty is using horses because he has such a weak following. He has his men, but aside from them he's apparently on his own. You don't hear about his constituents helping reassemble Humpty Dumpty. His family and advisers don't jump in either. This guy is not a leader, which causes him to use his contractually bound men and their helpless horses too. He's running an administration in decline and his handling of Humpty Dumpty is a prime example of that.

# Would you let Winnie the Pooh watch your kids?

In *The Jungle Book*, Mowgli is ten years old and has lived in the jungle his whole life. Bagheera is a panther who is biologically at most fifteen years old. Which one is smarter?

**Marry, coitus, kill: Holden Caulfield, Tom Riddle (young Lord Voldemort), Lady Macbeth?**

Dr. Seuss wrote two books about a race called the Whos: *Horton Hears a Who!* (in which the Whos live on a flower) and *How the Grinch Stole Christmas* (the location is never specified). Are they the same race? If so, does all the action in the Grinch story take place on a flower?

Would you rather be accepted to Hogwarts School of Witchcraft and Wizardry or Xavier's School for Gifted Youngsters?

Is the Muffin Man in the nursery rhyme a human man who makes muffins or an anthropomorphic muffin akin to the Gingerbread Man?

Would you rather read a Shakespeare play about the dawn of social media or the space race?

Do hobbits have tough, furry feet because they descended from tough-footed apes or because their ancestors didn't believe in shoes and natural selection weeded out all the soft-footed, hairless ones?

If a book could feel, would it rather you fold its page corners or shove a bookmark into it?

Who would be the most interesting replacement for Daisy Buchanan in *The Great Gatsby*: Amy Schumer, Nicki Minaj, or Angela Merkel?

Are Baby Bear's food and bed "just right" for Goldilocks because they are both children or is Baby Bear's preference the result of him being a genetic mix of Papa Bear (who prefers his bed hard and porridge hot) and Mama Bear (who loves her soft mattresses and cold gruel), making his tastes a balance of the two?

Who would fare best if he or she were thrust into the plot of *Lord of the Flies*: Lennie from *Of Mice and Men*, Scout from *To Kill a Mockingbird*, or Snowball from *Animal Farm*?

**If you were Cinderella, would you at some point try to explain to Prince Charming that your carriage was a pumpkin and your horses were actually mice, or would you lie about that throughout the marriage?**

Are the wizards in the Harry Potter universe descendants of apes or are they an alien species that can breed with humans?

In the story of "Rapunzel" a full-grown man climbs the tower using her hair. Does she have extraordinarily strong neck muscles or does her cell in the tower house a strong head brace?

If you were the main character in *The Scarlet Letter*, what letter would you rather wear everywhere: *F* for "Forwards chain conspiracy theory emails," *N* for "Never washes her hands," or *K* for "Kicks dogs"?

**Does Little Red Riding Hood mistake a wolf for her grandmother because her grandmother is extremely hairy or because Little Red Riding Hood is extremely nearsighted?**

Which *Wizard of Oz* character would you trust most to be president of the United States: the Cowardly Lion, the Tin Man, or the Scarecrow?

Would you rather live in the world of "Hey Diddle Diddle," where cats play music, cows jump over objects in space, and dishware runs away, or in the world of "There Was an Old Woman Who Swallowed a Fly," in which people eat cats and can unhinge their jaws and swallow cows whole?

**Did the old woman who lived in a shoe reside in a shoe the size of a house or were she and her children roughly the size of ants?**

Would Romeo and Juliet have gotten together if they had met on a dating site?

Who does more damage in "Hansel and Gretel": the witch, who tries to eat the children, or the birds, who eat the children's bread trail?

Is the Where's Waldo series about a secret agent who specializes in hiding in plain sight, or is it about a traveler who attends striped-shirt conventions around the world?

Would you rather suddenly wake up as a character in a horror novel you've read, or in a spy novel you haven't?

# FINE ARTS FOR DEEP THINKERS

Artists are geniuses. They combine beauty with precision, black spandex with berets. How do they do it? Where do they buy the paint? How do they learn to play piano? Is it actually them singing or is it a recording? These are questions no one can answer, so we don't ask them in this chapter. Rather, this tableau of questions gets to the very root of art. Here you'll look for the art inside selfies, the majesty inside Mario, and the porn inside paintings. Delve deeply enough and you'll become art yourself—something beautiful that asks questions about the world. Maybe the art was inside you all along!

If the Teenage Mutant Ninja Turtles and their artist namesakes were in a pizza-making contest, who would win?

**POINT:** The OG Leonardo, Donatello, Michelangelo, and Raphael clearly have the upper hand here. The TMNT are world-renowned for their shared love of pizza, but they begin with some severe disadvantages relative to Europe's great Renaissance artists. It's called artisan pizza, after all. If you can paint the ceiling of a chapel or give *Mona Lisa* that mysterious smile, you can get the cheese and pepperoni right. Plus, who in his right mind would trust a bunch of teenagers with an oven? With their hormones, trendy fads, and sweet flips and stunts, they are bound to burn that pizza.

**COUNTERPOINT:** To make a good pizza—a hot, delicious feast for the ages—you have to know the cuisine. The world's beloved Renaissance artists created masterpieces, not tasty slices. But the TMNT were raised on pizza. These green teens live by the way of the pie. There isn't a lot to eat in the sewers of New York City. Day in, day out, it is pizza. Through their immersion in that sweet saucy goodness, they learned the essence of the za. They could make it with their eyes closed, if they could close their eyes—which I'm not sure they can…

**Which character from the X-Men would be most useful at a bank heist: Professor X, Wolverine, or Magneto?**

Would the model for the *Mona Lisa* appreciate people spending five hundred years wondering what she's thinking?

Who is most likely to be the human manifestation of his or her namesake planet: Freddie Mercury, Venus Williams, or Bruno Mars?

Vincent van Gogh famously cut off his ear and sent it to a sex worker with whom he was enamored. If Van Gogh suddenly gave you his ear, would you be touched or terrified?

Is it better to paint with the legs of a tarantula or the tail of a horse?

If a raven takes a paintbrush in its beak and draws on a canvas, does that make it an artist?

Since Bugs Bunny and Daffy Duck can talk, should it be illegal for Elmer Fudd to hunt them?

Which painter's work would you rather reproduce using a paint-by-numbers kit: the messy drip paintings of Jackson Pollock or the detailed pointillism paintings of Georges Seurat?

Does farting loudly during a concert make you part of the show?

**Do the toys in Toy Story have parents?**

# Can a painting be porn?

Who would be better at *Tetris*: an architect who specializes in building walls or a demolition man who specializes in destroying them?

**Marry, coitus, kill: The Killers's Mr. Brightside, David Bowie's Major Tom, Chuck Berry's Johnny B. Goode?**

Would you rather have to dance whenever you speak or only be able to communicate by singing?

If Goofy and Pluto are both dogs, why does Goofy sleep inside and drive a car while Pluto sleeps in the yard and wears a collar?

Would more or fewer people play first-person shooter games if their enemies had the real faces of the other people playing against them?

Who would break more laws in modern America: Johnny Depp as Captain Jack Sparrow, Johnny Depp as Willy Wonka, or Johnny Depp as the Mad Hatter?

**Would people be as obsessed with the Venus de Milo if she still had her arms?**

Which animated animal is a better representation of its real-life version: Sonic the Hedgehog or the Tasmanian Devil?

Within the world of James Bond, is he one secret agent who is simply portrayed by multiple actors, or is he actually multiple secret agents who are given the name James Bond after the previous one dies?

# Does a selfie qualify as a self-portrait?

Which film has the most realistic aliens: *E.T.*, *Mars Attacks!*, or *Alien*?

Marry, coitus, kill: Fountains of Wayne's Stacy's Mom, Michael Jackson's Billie Jean, Dolly Parton's Jolene?

**Would Han Solo be better at pretending to be Indiana Jones or vice versa?**

Are Bart, Lisa, and Maggie Simpson's spiky heads made of skin-colored hair, or are the spikes an extension of their skin?

Pac-Man eats only white dots, ghosts, and fruit. Does that make him a vegetarian?

Would you rather be a passenger in a car with a first-time driver who has played thousands of hours of high-speed racing games or one who hasn't played any racing games at all?

Marry, coitus, kill: *Vitruvian Man, American Gothic, The Last Supper?*

Who would do better on *Jeopardy!* as a contestant: (Good) Will Hunting or Jason Bourne?

No written English words or letters appear in the Star Wars universe. So, how did the Rebel Alliance decide on the names for the X-Wing and Y-Wing?

If you insert movie quotes into conversation as though they're your own ideas, is it plagiarism or an homage?

Would it be better if The Beatles were all still alive and touring together if it meant that they never put out *Abbey Road*?

**Mickey Mouse only wears pants and Donald Duck only wears a shirt—which one is more naked?**

Who is better at
his job: Mario
at plumbing or
the Swedish Chef
at cuisine?

**Which Lord of the Rings character would have the most popular talk show: Gandalf, Bilbo, or Gollum?**

Would you be more or less likely to go to a Beastie Boys concert if they all dressed as Beast from the X-Men?

In the musicals of stage and screen, are the characters actually singing and dancing in real life or do the musical numbers only occur in their imaginations?

# Are Smurfs mammals, reptiles, insects, birds, or fungi?

Would you rather have sex with Carrot Top in Idris Elba's body or have sex with Idris Elba in Carrot Top's body?

# Marry, coitus, kill: the Wicked Witch of the West, Hannibal Lecter, Beetlejuice?

# Would Picasso enjoy Mr. Potato Head?

Would you rather watch *The Godfather* with all the characters played by Muppets or *The Departed* with all the characters played by M&M's?

# CHAPTER 5
## SOCIAL SCIENCES FOR
## DEEP THINKERS

Deep thinkers need social sciences to survive. The deeper you climb inside your own head, the harder it becomes to do social things, such as going outside in the daytime, making eye contact with your personal magician, or ordering food without pointing to your open mouth. Luckily, you have this chapter to guide you through the mysteries of social life. You just might uncover the secrets behind human behavior as you ponder the questions found here, such as the benefits of solid food versus baby food and whether or not you should feel awkward when you think about former child stars aging into attractive adults. Open your mind to the sweet science of society and become the best psycho-socio-economist on your block!

Is it more acceptable for a human being to eat a dolphin or for a pig to eat a human?

**POINT:** We have been treating pigs poorly for generations now. We ridicule them constantly. What's the worst thing you can call someone when he eats too much? A pig! We even put pictures of pigs eating themselves on barbecue billboards! So I say it's about time a pig gets its revenge. If some pig is crafty enough to find a way to dine on a human rather than the other way around, more power to the pig. Not only is it fair, it's actually pretty darn impressive.

**COUNTERPOINT:** Whose team are you on? At the end of the day, it's us or the beasts. I'm not saying it would be fun to eat a dolphin. They're smart, love to laugh, and would probably have rubbery meat. But they're not human! I've never understood why so many people side with animals over other people. You can't shake hands with a dolphin. You can't ask it to save you a seat at the movies. You can't take loving family pictures with it at Sears. What, do they think they're too good for us? It's high time they learned some respect. And nothing teaches something respect like eating it.

Suppose your life savings is assembled in a big stack of cash. Which would you rather have watching it: a family of crows or a robot with a tennis racket?

**How many friends need to sip from the same container before it's too gross to drink from?**

Would you rather kiss a person who has jelly beans for teeth or a banana for a tongue?

Would it be worse to be a middle schooler who says everything she thinks out loud or an adult who has to listen to middle schoolers' best insults of her every day until she dies?

Would the New York Stock Exchange be better if every broker on the floor sounded like Kim Kardashian or Ray Romano?

How long after a former child star turns eighteen does it become acceptable to admit being attracted to him or her?

# Is it bribery to give a kid an allowance for doing her chores?

Is it inhumane to make a baby cry for a movie?

**What's worse: tricking a child out of $10 or stealing $10 million from a billionaire?**

What's the most expensive item you can borrow and forget to return without it qualifying as stealing?

Marry, coitus, kill: the person who tries to strike up a conversation with you while your headphones are in; the guy who sings "Your Body Is a Wonderland" at karaoke; the student who comes back from studying abroad with an accent?

Who would you rather have a *Freaky Friday* body swap with for a day: Jay Leno, Jay-Z, or Jaden Smith?

How many people need to be waiting ahead of you before you're officially standing in a line?

**If you soak toast in water, is it still toast?**

Who is under more stress:
a Little League coach who
suspects one of his players
is actually an adult or a
professional coach who knows
one of his star players is
a bank robber?

If you had to do one thing every day for a year, which would you choose: texting the wrong person, saying "You too" after the waiter tells you to enjoy your meal, or walking behind somebody who's walking too slowly?

Would you accept $1,000 in pennies if you had to carry it around until you spent it all?

Is a bowl of undressed lettuce a salad?

**Would it be harder to play beach volleyball on your knees or only using your elbows?**

What would you rather wear at all times: flippers or a mask and snorkel?

**Would you rather eat a cloud or a crisp autumn leaf?**

Is it more inconsiderate to burn $50 from your grandma or throw away the birthday card it came in without reading it?

Would you rather eat meat from a seal or a penguin?

# Are checks money?

If human bodies grew as fast as those of other animals (but human brains took as long to develop as they do now), would children still go to school until age eighteen?

Which food would you trade out for its body part namesake: chicken fingers, angel hair pasta, or hamburger buns?

# Who could kill you more easily: an Olympic boxer or an Olympic javelin thrower?

If you could survive without one, would you rather never eat again or never sleep again?

Who is more deserving of receiving $1 million: somebody who won it by playing the lottery or somebody who inherited it?

Does a person look classier playing beer pong or bowling?

Would you rather eat the same meal of your choice for the rest of your life or an infinite variety of baby food?

Would it be easier to chew if your teeth were replaced with little wheels or tiny butter knives?

Which is a bigger
waste of money:
a sterling silver
wallet chain
or gold teeth?

Who would be better at delivering a baby: a football center (i.e., the guy who hikes the ball) or a soccer goalie (i.e., the guy who guards the net)?

**Whose transition would be more difficult: a totalitarian monarch who suddenly became an average citizen or an average citizen who suddenly became a totalitarian monarch?**

**Would you rather step on a Lego every time you walk or eat a side of Play-Doh with every meal?**

Who would be more likely to be a great athlete: a masochist or a sadist?

**Are you more likely to get mugged if you walk around wearing a bejeweled crown or a jacket made of $50 bills?**

Would it be better if you had to bow whenever anybody entered the room or if trumpets announced your entrance into any room?

# Does investing your money count as work?

# Who would be better at soccer: a person with three legs or a person without hands?

Marry, coitus, kill: poker champion, hockey champion, video game champion?

Would you rather be able to understand every language but have incomprehensible speech and writing, or be universally understood in every language but not understand any written or spoken words?

When you're sitting in a movie theater, which armrest is yours?

Would you rather have eyebrows so long that they cover your eyes or toenails so long that they stick out of your shoes?

**Would you rather have chopsticks for fingers or roller skates for feet?**

Who most deserves his or her face on digital currency: Steve Jobs, Chelsea Manning, or Morpheus from the Matrix movies?

**Which board game would be more terrifying to be trapped inside: Candy Land or Clue?**

Would you rather your government be run exclusively by people under age eighteen or over age eighty?

# Does a whole chicken breast on a hamburger bun qualify as a burger?

Would you rather ride in a car with a blindfolded driver or fly in a plane with a blindfolded pilot?

**Is it socially acceptable to talk to a server with your mouth full?**

# CHAPTER 6
## NATURAL AND APPLIED SCIENCES
## FOR DEEP THINKERS

Neil deGrasse Tyson once said that Albert Einstein once said that Marie Curie once said that Isaac Newton once said that science is really pretty neat. The beautiful thing about science is that every answer just brings more questions. Sure, you may know that the earth revolves around the sun, but do you know if *T. rexes* could play patty-cake? Do dogs realize when we're naked? Would cats notice if robots replaced us? So, be a deep thinker and do some science in this chapter: put forth a hypothesis, test it, and then let your friends tear it apart. Most days, that's just life. But today, it's science!

**Is turning off a computer closer to tucking it in for bed or killing it?**

**POINT:** Turning a computer off is like giving it a sweet little nap; there is no way it's akin to murder. A computer is truly dead only if you dump water on it and watch it fry out. Any other time it's simply sleeping and waiting to be used lovingly again. It's not like you're being malicious when you turn off a computer. Quite the opposite. It's an act of love that lets that hardworking processor rest its circuits. Turning a computer off comes from a place of care and love. That's why we all kiss our laptops gently every night when we turn them off.

**COUNTERPOINT:** When a computer is turned off, all signs of life disappear. Its fan stops moving. It stops surfing the Internet. Its videos stop playing midstream. In short, it is functionally dead. Why would a computer have a "sleep mode" if turning it off was just helping it sleep? You may say that because it can turn back on, it's not dead. But people are brought back from the dead all the time. What do you think those rub-em-together-and-yell-*clear* paddles are for?

**Have there been fewer UFO visits in recent years or have people stopped reporting them for some other reason?**

# Could two *T. rexes* play patty-cake?

How large does a rubber ducky have to be for it to be considered a boat?

# Which dinosaur is least likely to kill you?

**Would you rather drive through a city in a monster truck or in a car that walks on robotic legs?**

Which invention will future civilizations find the most useful: the radio, the pen, or the coin?

**What will human beings stop using first: cell phones or human surgeons?**

# Which dinosaur would make the best pet?

Why do aliens send their messages through cornfields and not, say, paper messages, digital messages, or radio?

**Which animal is most likely to actually be an alien: the octopus, the platypus, or the raven?**

Would we be as impressed by the planets if they were named after the Seven Dwarfs instead of Greek and Roman gods?

Would you choose to be the first person to land on another planet, even if you could never see or talk to another human being again?

If you attach two bicycles to each other and strap a jetpack to the back, is it a car?

Would the world's greatest soldier or a great white shark win in a fight in a backyard swimming pool?

**Marry, coitus, kill: invisible mad scientist, bioengineered human-animal hybrid, shape-shifting alien?**

**What's the best nine-to-five job for a dinosaur?**

Who would you rather send to space: a friendly acquaintance or a clone of yourself?

# Who will arrive at another planet first: humans or self-aware robots?

**What's a better mutation: an extra set of arms or 360-degree vision?**

Would you rather have houseplants that constantly insult you or grass that screams when you cut it?

# What's the most untrustworthy animal?

Which of our common ancestors better represents humanity: a microscopic organism that feeds on feces or a rodent that only eats baby dinosaur eggs?

Is it safer to walk across town on mechanical stilts that move continuously or traditional stilts that you move at your own pace?

How long would a prehensile tail have to be to become more inconvenient than helpful?

If a horse is born with a horn, would the other horses tease it for being different or revere it for being a unicorn?

Would you rather have upper-body hair thick enough that it looks like a shirt or lower-body hair thick enough that it looks like pants?

# Would you rather have two noses or no ears?

would be more
difficult to hide:
superstrength

If animals decide one day to turn against humanity en masse, who would win the ensuing war?

# Would dolphins build cities if they could?

# Do dogs realize when we're naked?

**If machines replaced all of humanity tomorrow but kept feeding cats, would cats notice or care?**

**Would you rather have a scorpion, a shark, or a tiger as a pet?**

If you had to pay
your pet to live
in your house and
play with you,
would you?

# Do apes know they're related to us?

# When the first human beings found dinosaur bones, what did they think they had unearthed?

Which would be a more dangerous animal hybrid: a scorpion-shark or a bat-cobra?

Is it more likely that crows are the ghosts of dead humans or spies from another dimension?

Would you rather have your eyes, ears, and mouth move a fraction of an inch toward your nose or away from it every year?

What's more human: going to the bathroom indoors or running without being chased/chasing something?

**Which invention better trains youngsters for the world: the yo-yo or the pogo stick?**

# Would dinosaurs be more or less dangerous if they could drive?

Are animals trying to talk to us when they make noise, and if so, are they frustrated that we never respond?

**What animal would handle life on the International Space Station best: a hummingbird, a bullfrog, or a narwhal?**

# ABOUT THE AUTHORS

Henry Kraemer is one half of the hosting duo for the hypotheticals comedy podcast *Wild Speculation* and the good-actors-in-bad-movies podcast *The Eh List.* A Portland, Oregon–based political activist and prankster whose exploits have been covered by *Time*, NPR, and *The Washington Post*, Henry is mildly infamous for saying sassy things to powerful people, prompting garbage-fire debates on social media, and raising a small dog who's universally recognized as more popular than him.

Brandon Marcus is the other half of the hosting duo for *Wild Speculation* and *The Eh List* and a spirited pop culture aficionado. Brandon's writing has appeared on several sites including Fandom.com, CHUD.com, and NerdBastards.com. He has been soaking in all things movie, TV, and music from a young age. He also spends his time complaining about politics, reading comics, and hopelessly rooting for his Los Angeles Lakers.